The Day I Lost My Bear in Cypress Hills

by Melanie Larson

illustrated by Kaustuv Brahmachari

M Larson Books

Saskatchewan, Canada

M Larson Books

Copyright M Larson

ISBN 978-1-7753218-5-9

All rights reserved.

No part of this publication may be reproduced or stored in a retrieval system, or transmitted in any form or by any means, electronic, mechanical, recording, or otherwise, without written permission of the publisher, M Larson Books, Saskatchewan, Canada. In the case of photocopying, a licence must be obtained from Access Copyright (Canadian Copyright Licensing Agency), 56 Wellesley Street West, Suite 320, Toronto, Ontario M5S 2S3 (1-800-893-5777) or visit www.accesscopyright.ca.

For my little bears in Cypress Hills

Hi, my name is Finn and I'm 5 years old. The day I lost my stuffie named "Bear" started like most days in Cypress Hills. Bear and I woke up in my Grandparents' log cabin. I got up, and my little brother Dez, and big brother Owen and I had porridge for breakfast. We were ready for a fun-filled day!

Soon it was time to go to swimming lessons at the pool. Mom and Dad packed our bathing suits and we rode our bikes there. Bear rode along in my backpack. Bear goes everywhere with me!

My new friends came in the pool with me for our swimming lesson. I liked doing the treasure hunt for toys under the water the most! I could see Bear relaxing in the beach bag with my towel.

After swimming, we decided to visit the museum next door. I got to see a cougar, a moose, and even a beaver dam. They were very neat animals but I was glad they weren't real!

It was time to do something a little more dangerous! My brother Owen and I went rock climbing and our little brother Dez went zip lining with Dad!

After our climbing adventure everyone wanted some ice cream. I love Bubble Gum ice cream the most. Maybe we will go mini golfing tomorrow!

Next we went to the beach at the lake! We played in the water and built sandcastles. We could see a moose across the lake! Mom had to shake all the sand off Bear when we were done.

Owen likes to hike so I ran along. We collected pine cones, sticks and bugs. Dez got to ride in the stroller, I think a squirrel was following him!

We went back to the cabin for a hot dog roast. We were hungry after our big day! It started to get dark. I was getting tired and I wanted to hold my Bear and look at the bright stars before bed. That's when I realized that Bear was missing!

We had to find my bear! I got so sad and thought I would never hold Bear again. I need my Bear to sleep! Where could he be? Mom and I searched high and low for Bear all over Cypress Hills.

I found him! Bear was laying on the hiking trail where we were earlier! I was so happy! Bear and I had a very big day and now it was time for bed. We were going to have another big day in Cypress Hills tomorrow!

Goodnight Bear!

Can you find these animals, native to Cypress Hills, somewhere in this book?

Cougar
Moose
Squirrels
Cormorant
Turkey vultures
White tailed deer
Bats
Leopard frogs
Spider
Monarch butterflies

Melanie Larson is a Mom of 3 and farm wife in rural Saskatchewan. Before creating children's books, Melanie worked as an Environmental Consultant all over Western Canada. Her 1st book is called "Count Them! 50 Tractor Troubles". She created it to help her children learn to count and spell to 50 while learning farm safety. Melanie and her family stay busy with tractor rides, playing hockey and adventures in Cypress Hills Provincial Park.

Kaustuv Brahmachari is an animator and children's book illustrator. He grew up in a small town in West Bengal, India. He is the owner of an animation company named Fx and Color Studio. He has many clients from all over the world and he has been working with many of them for years doing his dream job.

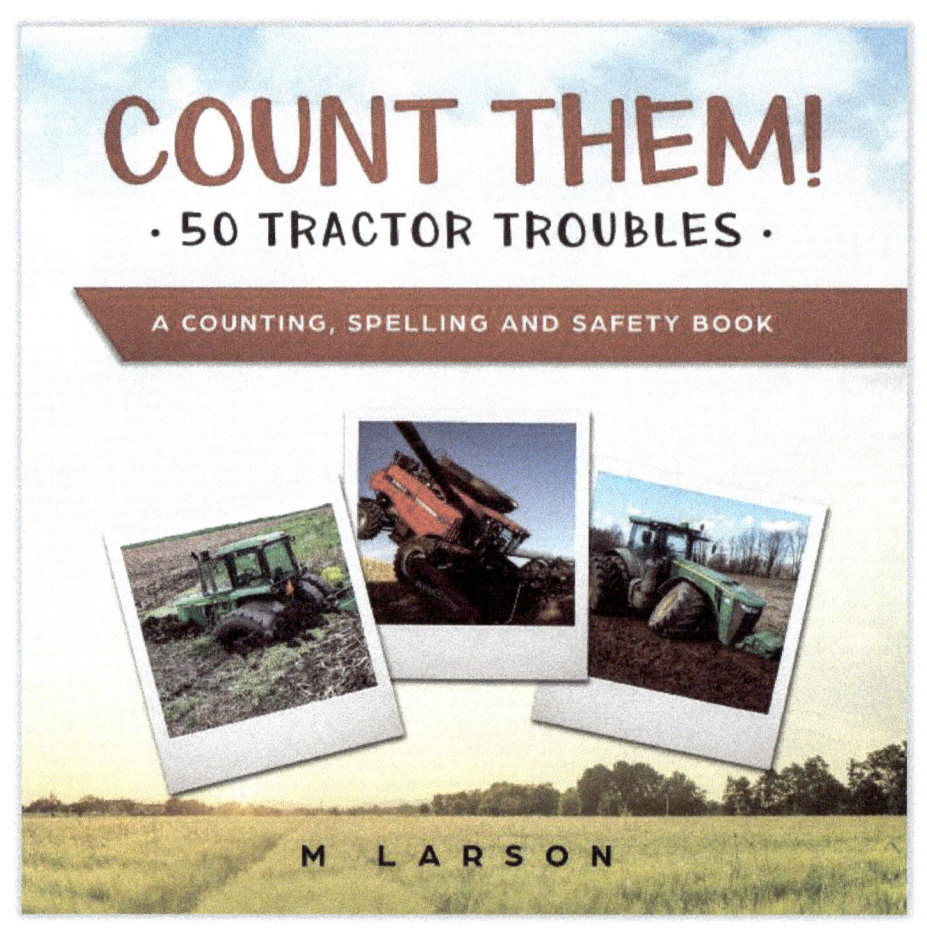

Count Them! 50 Tractor Troubles;
A Counting, Spelling and Safety Book

M Larson

available everywhere

www.ingramcontent.com/pod-product-compliance
Lightning Source LLC
Chambersburg PA
CBHW051301110526
44589CB00025B/2909